Be The
Fruitful Tree

Musa C Mobongwa

Musa Mobongwa

To order more copies of the book or to book the author as a
speaker call Musa Cyril Mobongwa on 071 416 9129 or
trosprojects@gmail.com.

Published by Manifest Publishing
www.manifestingthesons.com

Dedication

I dedicate this book to my mother Makhosazane G Mobongwa who became strong enough to raise us with responsibility, love and care after my father passed away

Table of Contents

Acknowledgments

I couldn't have written this book without the inspiration of the Holy Spirit. He is my great leader and I thank Him for bringing forth good fruit in my life.

I would like to thank my mother who has supported me thus far in everything, and especially in the writing of this book, 'Be The Fruitful Tree'. As a matter of fact, she is the one who appreciates my work the most. I thank her for believing in my abilities as her son. I thank my siblings who also motivated me to see this project through to the end.

I thank my pastor, Apostle N.E Ngoveni, for being a father who is able to raise up giants in the Kingdom. I thank his wife, Pastor Alicia Ngoveni, and Impact House Ministries for the impact you have made in my life.

I would also like to thank everyone who has helped me to complete this book.

Musa Mobongwa

Foreword

*B*e The Fruitful Tree by Musa C. Mobongwa is a piece of work that addresses the key aspects of being a tree that yields fruit in accordance with the will and purpose of God.

In Matthew 11:12-13 we read an account of Jesus Christ being hungry and seeing a fig tree in leaf from a distance. He goes to the tree to get some fruit but finds none. We learn from this passage that from a fruit tree - fruits are always expected. It was with expectation that Jesus approached the fig tree. A tree is seen from a distance by its leaves. We too are perceived according to our presentation, hence the statement "first impressions last." The disappointment of Jesus in finding no figs on a fig tree despite the fact that it was not its season is clearly evident on reading the account. A lesson to learn from this is that even in moments where we may think it is not our season, fruit (results) is expected from us.

Therefore being a fruit tree, the environment has an expectation of fruits from you, as a child of God, post finding your purpose on earth you need to equip yourself with knowledge that will help you yield fruits in and out of season. Eventually Jesus curses the fig tree because it had no fruit. It is important that we often undergo self introspection to assess if we not operating under curse. Operating under a Blessing it is by the grace of God, thus it is vital that we seek and live in His grace.

As a tree you need to understand that for you to be in shape and be fruitful, pruning will have to take place, water and sunshine are essential for you. What does this mean? In life we live and respect everyone but it is not everyone we need to accomplish our vision. There will be things that need to be cutoff, people or friends to let go and practices/traditions to be stopped, such as gossip, some music, or even refrain from reading certain material, as long as they are not adding value to your vision. The pruning process may seem like a loss up until new better branches develop. Sunshine and water represents God's Grace and Word in your life, they are the most important elements to propel your growth. Live under His grace, absorb and be the doer of His word, then your fruits are guaranteed.

A tree can also have various functions, such as working as a shade, as a log of wood for fire or even refined for paper manufacturing. However these are not the primary reasons a fruit tree exists, but secondary functions that every tree can perform. There are practices that can be done by a majority like being a follower, mind you the number of spectators always outnumbers that of players. The fruit will always advocate for the tree. By seeing and tasting the fruit, you will be able to tell if it comes from a good or bad tree. Read this book and learn how to be a fruitful tree, there is always more in life.

Minister Thulani Kwinana
Impact House Ministries

Musa Mobongwa

Endorsements

I have had many coaching sessions with Musa Mobongwa. I remember him teaching me to stay positive in mind and in action to obtain positive results. Mr Mobongwa and I also had a very fruitful coaching session concerning my business. We discussed team building and the power of teamwork for a successful business. As far as I know he is someone who is always positive, motivated, spiritually inclined, and hard working individual. Musa is someone I have known for many years and he has also been my spiritual mentor for a long time. When he started writing this book he mentioned it to me and I can confidently recommend it because I know his spiritual commitment and the special grace that rests upon him in the area of empowerment.

Kamohelo James Mofokeng
David Goliath International; Life Coaching Student

I have known Musa Mobongwa for a long time. I have found him to be generous, dedicated, determined, and self-driven. Another characteristic that has stood out for me is that he is very positive minded and always willing to help others achieve their dreams. No matter how hard things may seem, he doesn't change his mind to adapt to the situation but instead works hard and smartly to turn things around. Musa is a man of understanding and can be trusted as a life coach, motivational speaker and spiritual mentor.

Lebogang Matlapeng; Life Coaching Student

Introduction

I'm fruitful and you are fruitful. We are all God's creation - designed to be excellent and fruitful to God in everything we do and in everything we touch. The Bible says in Genesis 1:28, "God blessed them and said 'be fruitful and multiply'." We have been pursued by His blessings from the day we were formed till today. We are His candidates for blessing and His ambassadors for the promotion of His work. We are the ones who are carrying on with His work on earth and completing what He started.

He saw that we did not have what it took to carry out His works but wanted to use us regardless of our weaknesses. Because of this He decided to look at us through the eyes of faith rather than through our works. I can picture Him sitting on the throne with Jesus on His right hand, looking at us with eyes full of grace and love saying, "I won't bless this people through their works but I'll bless this people through faith in my Son."

When I go to God, I go as a child so that He can listen to me better and favour me without limitations. One day I went to buy bread in Roodepoort C.B.D. In front of me in the shop, queuing to pay for their purchases, was a lovely family with a young son of about four years of age. Their child took a chocolate bar off the shelves without permission and they noticed him chewing nonstop. On closer inspection the father noticed that the chocolate bar that they had not paid for had been opened and bitten. He shook his wife's shoulder silently to show her what was happening behind their backs. In fear the mother loudly said to the child, " Hey! What are you doing? You want to get us arrested?" She aggressively grabbed the chocolate out of the child's hand and paid for it. The child became nervous and started to cry. When he did this his father said, "Be quiet! I'm going to discipline you." On hearing these words the child was saddened and kept quiet instantly. Instead of crying further, he lifted up his hands indicating that he wanted to be picked up. The father picked him up and kissed him on the forehead while the mother was busy making payment for their purchases.

That is the attitude God is expecting from His children when they approach Him. Even when we feel like we are not good enough to serve Him, we must look beyond our mistakes and lift our hands in surrender to Him - always praying that He will pick us up. When we fail Him we don't stop being His children. We still qualify to do what sons do. Sons run their father's company and we qualify to do the same for God. He uses us because we avail ourselves as sons and not because we are perfect in His eyes. We are all called to be fruitful and we are all encouraged to stand tall. If there's someone looking down upon themselves, it might just be that we caused them to feel that way through our words and actions towards them.

We must bring forth good fruit so that we can build fruitful people in the church. God commanded us to be fruitful and multiply spiritually, financially and physically. I promise you that after reading this book your life will never be the same again. I took three whole years speaking to God about this topic and He gave me these revelations to share with you so that we can all bear good fruit. A man of God once said, "If I preach for you I preach for me also and if I build you I build myself also." We must believe that we are going to be restored in God.

This book reveals how we can become more fruitful in the areas of financial, spiritual and physical growth. God is able to restore all stolen seeds and He is entrusting you with His works that must be performed supernaturally for His people. This book *"Be the Fruitful Tree"* will teach you how to persist with your dream in Christ Jesus till you make it to your destination. It will take you from 1% to 100% without making you feel condemned or judged. You will be empowered spiritually and financially as you practice what is written in these Bible-inspired pages.

It's time to start believing what God has said about your life instead of what the enemy says about you. This book confirms the blessing that is upon our lives as God blessed mankind to be fruitful. This book resonates with the blessings of God. Get excited for you are about to be restored to the image of God and experience the blessing in your life. It feels so good to contemplate what God is about to do in your life after the reading of this book.

One day I was sitting in church listening to a man of God as he was preaching. He said that, "God blesses His people according to the knowledge they possess." I have found that to be true. If you want to be fruitful you must study fruitfulness. The Bible also says in Hosea 4:6 that God's people perish because of lack of knowledge. This verse shows us that knowledge is power, especially knowledge of the Word of God.

One thing I have learnt in this journey is that God is fulfilling His Word in us. I say "in us" because the Word must be in you so that you can be powerful and fruitful everywhere you go. God said to Joshua, "I give you this book of the law to meditate on it day and night so that you may prosper everywhere you go." The Word in you is life and is God in you. The same Word in you will make you fruitful. The plan of God was to plant the seed of prosperity in Joshua's life by the Word which was written. In the same way you can also be unstoppable by reading books that are written according to the will of God which is the Bible. The Word is very powerful especially if you give yourself time to meditate on it day and night. When you meditate you actually water the Word of God in you so that it takes deep root in your life for your own fruitfulness' sake.

That is God's method for preparing us for the blessing. The book of Isaiah confirms the same thing. "My word shall never return void." That is the promise of God to someone who walks by faith and is full of the Word. God listens attentively when we utter His Word in faith and in confidence. There is a song that I love to sing when I am alone. The words of the song are, "We lift Him higher for when the praises go up, His glory comes down". If you bless God through His word, He will come down and lift you up with the same measure you lift Him up. It will be in accordance with the measure of the knowledge of His Word that you possess and the measure with which you bless Him. If He is fruitful then you also are fruitful as He is your pillar. If He says, "I'm the true vine and you are the branches," it means that He bears fruit through us so that we can take responsibility for it and enjoy its flavour.

When He gives you a task it means that He wants to bring forth some new fruit through you. I'll advise you by saying, "Don't find yourself missing out on an opportunity to bear fruit in Christ Jesus no matter what. Now is your chance to read this book to the very last page so that you can bring forth good fruit.

Chapter One
Be Fruitful

I remember back in the days in the Free State province in South Africa, in a location called "Qwa Qwa", my friend Tankiso and I were sitting down under the cool shadows of the trees. We were sitting on bricks and talking about everything. Eventually the conversation turned to our future. I asked him where he saw himself in six years' time as I ate a succulent peach. My mouth was moving and the sweetness was satisfying my craving. I was holding a table knife in one hand with which I was busy pealing peaches. Tankiso answered me by asking, "Why?" as he threw some small stones at some birds that were singing on top of our heads in the trees.

In my heart I was burning with a desire to do something about my life. I continued to ask, "Man, I'm just asking what your vision is?" He said, "Musa man, whatever comes my way is fine. I'm not going to bother myself with dreams and visions that I'm not even sure I'll reach." I was young but I realised that he didn't have direction. He was lacking ambition. If you come across someone who doesn't have direction - who is hopeless - you must know that they need help. We don't judge people; we pray for them. I could see that Tankiso was someone without a seed of fruitfulness in his heart. If you say 'whatever comes my way,' you are simply saying, "I'm a garden that is ready to conceive any seeds that will fall on me".

Conceive Good Seed

In life, not all the seeds that fall on the garden soil are good seeds. Some are poisonous and some are good. Some can even destroy the garden. Be fruitful. Give birth to new dreams, new ideas, new songs, new hobbies, new movies, new promotions.... Renew your mind. Allow God to plant new seed in your heart. Don't receive bad seed. Be discerning about what you receive.

Don't be comfortable walking around with Tankiso's mindset. Don't be ignorant or be a person with no vision. You will need to look deep into your inner self and search your heart to discover what manner of seed God has planted in you. Be faithful to yourself and make proper self-introspection. Search your spirit and your heart. When you find something you want to excel in - take it and write it down.

This is the time to improve yourself in God so that you can be fruitful. Avail yourself to God and to someone you trust. Speak it out and be honest with your heart about it.

Write your dream down and meditate on it. Build up faith in it and forgive those that have wronged you in the past because you can't allow old pains to keep you from your promised land. I know that our pasts are different but don't ever give up and don't throw in the towel. If you are discouraged what you need is more encouragement. After discovering your purpose, make sure you find the help that you need. Avoid pride and humble yourself. You will be favoured everywhere you knock. Humble yourself before God and don't be boastful.

> *If my people which are called by my name, shall humble themselves, and pray, and seek my face, and turn from their wicked ways; then will I hear from heaven, and will forgive their sin, and will heal their land.*
>
> *2 Chronicles 7:14*

Humble Yourself Before God

There was a man who was married to his beautiful wife. He had a house next to where we were renting property in the north side of Roodepoort. He just liked to go out and drink. He thought that he could solve anything by drinking. One day he said, "Musa my friend, I feel good when I am drunk because I forget all my pain and suffering." I am talking about someone who has a very good, well-paying job, which had been his dream for many years. One morning he had a very bad argument with his wife and decided to one small bottle of brandy to ease his anger and stress before he went to work.

Driving to work, he got into a minor crash at a robot before he could reach his destination. My friend was already drunk. Just imagine being drunk early in the morning on your way to work. He crashed with a company car that morning before seven o'clock. My friend didn't have a choice but to call his bosses soon after the nightmare. He saw that He was already late and his bosses were going to make a case out of his late coming. They came to the scene to investigate the matter. His alcohol consumption levels were tested and he was found to be drunk. They fired him for drunk driving and negligence.

I used to sit with that guy sometimes and talk about business. He was always telling me that he could only deal with anger when he drank alcohol. You see what I'm talking about! This is a sign that he was aware of the situation. He knew deep in his heart that he had a problem that he needed to solve but decided to be stubborn and prideful. He mistakenly thought that by forgiving his wife he would be doing her a big favour. What he needed was for someone to let him know that the world did not revolve around him. He should have surrendered and gained forgiveness in Christ Jesus instead of turning to alcohol. His mind needed to be renewed.

He needed a new mind - a fruitful mind in Christ Jesus. Most people think alcohol, drugs and pleasures can solve their problems or at least control their anger and pain. That's not true. I'm here to tell you that they are going to make your problems even worse than before. It's only God who can solve all of your problems. My friend needed to get to the root of the problem and admit that he really needed help from a professional counselor or the Spirit of God Himself for the situation that he was in. It is not my intention to judge or to condemn. None of us are perfect. We must learn to listen to our hearts and allow the Holy Spirit to humble us so that we can be corrected and helped for our own betterment. If you know you have a problem that will disturb you from bearing fruit, it's time that you deal with it.

Seek God's Help To Be Set Free From Your Burdens

I know it sounds stupid or unnecessary sometimes, but to God it is necessary. He has sent authors, pastors, life coaches, and mentors for our sake - to help us. Everyone who has a car takes it to the mechanical engineers for fixing when it develops a problem. The experts will first locate the problem then tell you the solution. It is the same with your life's problems. You must take your mind and your spirit straight to God so that He can reveal your problem and fix it for you. He is always there for you and me so that we can get help. You must take your problems to God. It is a good thing to try to manage your mind by reading good books, going to church, spending time with your life coach or mentor, or visiting your doctor, but the most important thing is to build a strong relationship with God above.

We should always humble ourselves and be able to approach people who can help us. None of us are perfect and we all need to walk with someone who knows better than we do. God is available to those who avail themselves to Him. Humble yourself so that you can get some fruitful results. Avoid pride by all means. It's very dangerous and produces the fruit of death. It can kill your relationships with your family and other loved ones. It can take your job from you and even destroy your business and dreams. If you are full of pride no one will consider you for opportunities that come up. Good seed is conceived from the Word of God.

You must be discerning about what you conceive, what you drink and what you eat. Learn from the pregnant woman. She doesn't just eat and drink everything that comes her way because she knows that not all is good for the baby. Your personal dream is your own child - your own seed or offspring - that you are going to give birth to in the fullness of time. Make sure you don't consume anything that will destroy your future. When you plant a seed in the garden you don't throw or pour anything on the garden soil or on the seed itself that might reduce it's potential to grow well in the future.

If you want to walk in victory or in God's plan, you must spend a lot of time listening to the Holy Spirit. Whatever the Spirit wills, jump and say, "Yes Lord! I am what You say. I am here Holy Spirit. I am the fruitful tree. I am what God says I am. I am fruitful and prosperous in everything I touch." In the book of Exodus 3:14 Moses asks God, "If these people ask me who sent me what must I say?" God said, "Tell them "I am that I am has sent you".

God lives in me and also in you. Christ lives in us so that we can adopt His character and do as He does and talk as He talks. We don't live for ourselves but for Christ who owns our hearts. The Spirit of God lives in us to activate and stir up His power and love in us so that we can walk in victory. Jesus empowered us with His Word which is spirit and truth. Everything positive and healthy that you feel about yourself is true so don't be apologetic or afraid to take back what belongs to you by fire and by force.

Paul says in the book of 2 Timothy 1:7, "He didn't give us the spirit of fear but of power, love and of a sound mind." God expects us to walk in power, love and confidence so that we can possess all that God has promised us from within our spirits. Believe in God and also in yourself as the fruitful tree, planted by God who commanded you to "be fruitful".

My Portion is to Agree With God in Me.

If I say I am what God says I am, I agree with Him. "Yes" I am what the Spirit in me is confessing about me. If the Spirit in me says I am fruitful then I have the right to confirm it and act it till it manifests in the physical realm. "I Am" in me has declared my destination as the fruitful tree. If "I Am" in me speaks and says I am the fruitful tree, I can't say "no" because "I Am" who speaks in me is God Himself speaking through the Spirit in me. I must stand tall and say, "I am the fruitful tree". Don't be apologetic especially when the spirit declares victory in you. Just stand tall and say, 'I am."

Do you know that if you stand in the classroom and say, "I am a teacher," automatically children will want to learn from you and they will also start to give you a teacher's respect. In return they will expect you to deliver what a teacher delivers. The Word of God teaches that what a man speaks comes from the bottom of his heart and that what he thinks in his heart is what he is. You are what you speak and your introduction reveals your true self. Your first introduction is spiritual because people can feel the spiritual environment around you.

I am what my heart says about me. If the spirit in me declares me as healed then, "I am healed." If the spirit in me declares me as strong then, "Yes, I am strong." If the spirit in me declares me as beautiful then, "Yes, I am beautiful." If the spirit in me declares me as talented then, "Yes, I am talented." I and the spirit in me are one. You can't separate me from my spirit man. By declaring the words 'I am', you are positioning yourself to be who you say you are. Your mind and your actions will start to align themselves with what you always confess about yourself.

You become what you plant in your heart, eventually! By speaking to yourself in "I am" form, you eventually plant a seed in your heart. Don't just say it; believe in your heart you're your mouth is confessing. If you are not sure yet of your destiny take the opportunity to start calling yourself by your talents. If your talent is singing, start to call yourself a musician. Record demo CDs and start performing. Turn your hobby into a career. Start acting like a musician. Meditate on it day and night and speak it out loud till it takes root. Plant that seed in your heart and not only in your mind. Imagine it and confess it. Act it, feel it, and you'll see it coming your way.

Pray, Speak And Act Till You See Results

There is a guy I know by the name of Mfanelo. We grew up together in Qwa Qwa and he relocated to Johannesburg five years before I did. For as long as I'd known him he had always dreamt of becoming the manager of a clothing shop. He found a job in one of the big clothing shops in Roodepoort and worked hard. Every time we met he would tell me that he would soon be a manager. From looking at him it was obvious that he could both see and feel the reality of himself as a manager in his heart. He was even starting to behave like a manager already. "I am going to be the manager," was his constant confession.

One year passed without the promotion to manager but he maintained his confession despite the disappointments he was facing. The years kept passing by until he was approaching seven years without the promotion. He still kept confessing that he was going to be a manager. He still saw himself as a manager and God answered his prayers. That is how it works. God watches your hard work and rewards you according to the work of your hands, your heart and passion.

People can laugh at you, gossip about you, and try to discourage you. Some might even stoop to mocking you when you walk by saying, "Here comes the dreamer." They focus only on the disappointments you are facing without any awareness of what God is about to do in you. You must not focus on what people are trying to plant in your heart. You are more than a conqueror through Christ our Lord. Jesus says, "All things are possible if you believe".

God would like to see you believing in Him for every difficulty you are facing so that He can lift you up. He only wants the best for you. You are His candidate to carry out His good works on Earth. You are the tree that carries God's fruit in Christ Jesus. By doing what your spirit says through Christ Jesus your life will never be the same again. Be like Elijah when He was praying for rain. You must pray for the rain to fall on you till you see the results. Pray till you see the signs. Don't give up even if the world is battling against your call. Hold on until you see the cloud. When it starts to drizzle don't stop praying. It's just the start. Don't pay attention to the negative words people around you are speaking against your vision but choose to focus on your promised fruit like Mfanelo did. He waited for seven years without giving up.

I'm sure it wasn't easy for him to hold on and we all feel weary sometimes. That is why the Lord told us in Habakkuk 2:2 to "write the vision and make it plain." He said that because people give up quickly. Everything you write down, read and meditate upon becomes part of you.

I believe in reading and writing and it's working for me. Sometimes our dreams are so large that they look like a fantasy and we tend to forget them. We have to realise that all our dreams come from God. It is He who has put them in our hearts and spirits through the grace and love He has for us. His will is to make us fruitful so we must work with Him not against Him. We are His children - His branches - and we will bear fruit in partnership with Jesus Christ through all the trials and tribulations we face for His glory. As we are fruitful branches in Him we will face attacks from pests that want to feed on us but God won't allow them to destroy us because whoever is destroying us destroys His mission in us. Whoever touches us touches God.

Chapter Two

The Fruitful Branches

In the fifteenth chapter of the book of John we see Jesus teaching us about the tree and the branches. He teaches that He is the true vine, we are the branches and God is the vineyard owner. Jesus says, "Every branch that holds on to me, my father will prune so that it can bear more fruits. Those who are not attached to me will be dry and my father will gather them and throw them in the fire." This should not make you feel condemned for there is no condemnation to those who attach themselves to Him. You and I are fruitful because we are attached to Him. He is our provider of grace and He made us to be fruitful. He gave us all that we need in His name. We are the fruitful branches.

When I was young I had a friend named Sedisa in primary school. I want to tell you about an incident that took place when he was ten years old and I was nine years old. We were walking home from school one sunny day when we passed by a fenced house full of peach trees. The peaches were ripe and red and all of the branches were hanging. Our mouths were watering from the sight of them.

At our home we had peach trees and before that day I thought we were rich in peaches. That day I realised that we had to plant more of our apricot and peach trees. It was clear that we needed to expand our territory. After seeing that yard we were inspired to do more than before. We started to collect more apricot seeds. I remember that day like it was yesterday. We didn't play anymore because of the mission we had. I decided to invite Sedisa to my place so that we could begin our project of planting more trees. We were so determined and busy working our ground that he didn't even go home that day. Just imagine it; we were both still in our school uniform. We wanted to plant our seeds as quickly as possible before we could get into trouble with our mothers. His mother was at work and mine was out of town. You should have seen how dirty our uniforms how were.

My school trousers were wet and soiled with garden soil because I was digging holes with a small garden scoop. Sedisa would follow behind me with some seeds. He would toss the seeds in the hole, I would cover the seed with garden soil and he would water the seed to conclude the process. Sometimes he would accidentally spray me with water. My shoes gave the impression that I had been playing in a muddy puddle. I can't tell you what my mother did to me that day! Today, when I go home we are still eating peaches and apricots from those trees. Even the birds are sitting on their branches. Some seeds didn't make it but others did and became fruitful trees. It is the same with people; some make it and others don't.

You must allow yourself to be inspired by other people who are more skilled than you or who have achieved more so that you can be more fruitful. Attach yourself to fruitful people. If you can't find any nearby make an plan. You can buy their DVDs and books or follow them on their social media platforms.

What Kind of a Branch Are You?

Dry or fruitful? We are fruitful with no doubt. We are attached to Him and that is why everything we touch prospers. He gives us confidence to walk and stand tall, He gives us hope so we don't give up and He encourages us to keep knocking on closed doors.

People who know me will tell you that Musa can start anything anytime. Yes, I'm not afraid. I can do anything anytime because I know that I start in Him and I finish in Him. I fall in Him and I stand up in Him. His name is Jesus Christ. I'm not a failure. When I fall, there's always another chance to stand up again. The Word of God says that a righteous man falls several times but he still stands up again and again. I'll try it the first time, the second time and even the third time. I won't look back but will keep marching forward. I will keep pressing towards the future because the future is calling my name. I don't walk by sight but I walk by faith. I'm a fruitful tree without a doubt.

One day I was in Johannesburg CBD trying to buy something for myself in a certain shop I like. While I was busy inspecting the jeans, my phone rang. I wasn't comfortable answering it because the shop was too full and noisy with music playing from the roof. I needed to find a quiet corner where I could communicate better with my caller.

The call was from a friend of mine calling to catch up. He was also in Johannesburg CBD in the shop across the road from where I was. He suggested that we meet in a fast food restaurant nearby. We met and greeted each other with joy. He was wearing sunglasses and drinking sparkling water. On inspection, my friend was still the same as I remembered him. He is a person that I know to be fruitful and powerful. Whatever he touches prospers.

We ordered our food and all was well. I hadn't started writing this book at that time. We relaxed and I shared my vision that I was going to write a book. He looked straight in my face and asked sarcastically, "You Musa? A book?" I replied with a smile and full of confidence, "Yes". I could read his mind and could tell that he was taken aback. He asked, "Why a book?" I told him that I wanted to change people's lives. He nodded his head like he was agreeing with me then asked, "Where is that coming from?" He was so surprised that his eyes were round with amazement. He even took off his sunglasses so he could look at me closely. He knew there was no one in our circle who could have inspired me to come up with that idea. We didn't know anybody who was writing books. It didn't bother me though because I knew that God had a plan and would send people to show me the path.

I said, "I know I always call you when I'm in need of connections, but don't worry about this one. It comes from God Himself and He will provide me with the connections when the time is perfect". He laughed at me and said, "Good luck, but I'll support you once it is published." I knew that it was a new thing in our environment. I said "Sometimes the seed must come from God Himself. He will provide me with some connections."

I don't have anyone to lean on or to follow. I don't have anyone around me who is an author. My friends are not authors. My family are not authors and neither are my neighbours. I don't know anyone around me who is an author but I know the grace of God and His favour shall follow me for the rest of my life. If you do something do it perfectly so that it can give you confidence and hope. Do it with excellence so that others will want to be part of it.

If I Have God, I Have It All

I know God has confidence in my ability to bear good fruit because I am a branch that draws life from Jesus himself. He will provide the right people at the right time. I know that He wants the best for me. He has confidence in me and you the same way. That is why He prunes and prepares me first, before He can use me for His purposes. He can use me for new things in my community, at my place of work and for my country, because I am His good branch bearing His fruits.

He uses me not because I'm better than anybody else but because I chose Him as my provider and master. I believe in Him fully and He will continue using me and you for anything that He wants to do in the city. You are that good candidate for His good plans. He can never do anything without you. He counts on you for His work in the world to be done and He knows that His excellence will manifest through you.

If you do something, do it as if God is around as your supervisor. Don't wait for your bosses or your leaders to push you before you can do it - love it, practice it, and own it. If you are a worshipper, worship like God would. If you are a preacher, preach like God would. If you are an actor, act like God would. Forget about yesterday and focus on the future and on what you are doing because you can never be perfect on your own. He will prune you and perfect you. Don't allow the devil to confuse you. Jesus told his disciples that they were clean because of the Word that He had taught them. The Word still cleanses us and prepares us to carry out His work. Don't wait for tomorrow.

I believe that I'm more than a conqueror and nothing will stand in my way as long as I move with Him. I qualify because there is no condemnation to those who trust in the Lord. If He says, "I'm calling you for this," don't say, "I can't talk right. I don't have confidence. I'm not really good enough at this and that." He knows you. He knows everything about you. He knows your past and your future. He doesn't use perfect people but He uses the obedient and humble people like you. He chose you for Himself so no one can disqualify you. No one can curse what God has blessed. You are blessed going in and blessed going out. You are fruitful in everything you do.

I was with one of my faithless friends one day when he said to me, "Musa, if you - who believes in God - are facing these hard challenges, why must I believe in God or be born again? We are almost the same." I answered him this way, "God will continue allowing me to face some challenges and He won't stop testing my faith by letting them come my way. He has faith in me and knows that I'll overcome them. He also fights my battles." I went on to say, "All things work together for good to those who love the Lord. He has given us hope and everlasting power".

People will always view things and situations differently from others. Others view challenges as situations to destroy them or as fire to burn them to ashes. Some view challenges as stepping stones - as fire to cook them and prepare them for their mission. Others view challenges as part of life. I like challenges because they help me to grow and they are the pathway to the testimony.

You shall receive according to your expectations. If you entertain fear it will become your snare but if you have faith it will become your sword. If I were you, I would start planting the good seed of faith and expect good fruits from it. You reap what you sow. Poisonous seeds give birth to poisonous fruit and poisonous fruit kills. Healthy fruit gives life and prosperity. If challenges and storms come your way, just stand still and look up to Him. You are a branch connected to Him and destined for victory.

"I'm the tree that is rooted in Christ Jesus. I hold on to God's Word which is Jesus Christ because I'm a born again Christian full of the Holy Spirit. There is no need to complain about the storms and fires that arise in my life because I am a tree protected by my master. In times of trouble I look to God my heavenly Father. I am a living testimony that I'm a fruitful tree.

Let me tell you about my life. I have experienced unemployment, rejection, pains, and hard times. I have lost people I loved in my life and I have faced storms but I always say, "Here I am today and I'm better than yesterday. I'm proud to be me because now I can worship God better. I can now tell someone about God better." He delivered me from the storms and fires because I'm the tree that is holding on to the master. There is nothing I can do without my master's protection. He loves me and waters me when I am dry. He prunes me for my future. He protects me from the locusts and animals who would feed on my fruits and destroy my life. He has given me a reason to stand by faith in Him. He promised that He will save me and protect me. He promised that His plans are not to harm me but to prosper me.

Every situation tends to turn out exactly the way you expect it to. The Bible puts it this way, "Life and death is in the power of the tongue and those who love it will enjoy its fruits." God has put you in charge of your own situation and given you His Word and a tongue to speak and declare yourself better than before. What you say in the midst of the storms takes root and it will blossom. If you plant fear and expect defeat it shall blossom and give birth to deadly fruit. Don't be surprised when it takes root and grows to give birth to problems because you will be receiving the results of the seed that you were planting in your mind while you were in the middle of storms and fires. You are the one who planted it in your heart then it took root and blossomed.

It is the same with good seed. You shall go out with victory and glory. Speak well of yourself. You don't need money to speak words of favour over your life. Just say, "Surely goodness and mercy shall follow me all the days of my life." Plant the seed that will give birth to joy and victory and be the fruitful tree.

Make Yourself Useful

We are bound to be useful because we are the fruitful branches connected to Christ Jesus. We are purposed to carry fruits that will be useful to those around us. Avail yourself to Christ Jesus as a branch with great potential or ambition. We are connected to Christ and we don't lean on our own understanding but on Christ Jesus who is our heart's desire and pillar of strength.

With Christ we lack nothing. He is Lord and He is the master of everyone who gives Him glory and says, "Lord I'm what I am because of You." We are more than conquerors through Christ our Lord. We are the chosen generation, chosen to operate under His Spirit of life. We shall live in the spirit as fish live in water. When you take a fish out of the water it dies.

We must grow our faith in Him till we know that there is nothing we can do without Him. Our confidence is in Him who started the good work in us and who will also take it to the end. When I look back in my life to all the trials I have overcome it is clear that I would not have survived them without His wisdom and protection.

He Restored My Future and Vision

I can make a list of the things I didn't deserve but was given by the grace of Christ. It doesn't matter how many businesses you already have or how old you are. Like Abraham who received a child at one hundred years of age through Sarah who was ninety years old you can also be fruitful in your old age.

Chapter Three
You Shall Know The Tree By Its Fruits

My friend Thabo told me about an interesting game that he used to play with his cousins. They would be blindfolded and have to pick a piece of fruit from a fruit salad bowl. Points were scored by correctly identifying the type of fruit they were eating relying only on their senses of taste.

You can tell what manner of person someone is in the same way that you can distinguish between fruit. You use your tongue and sense of taste to know what fruit you are eating. With a human being you would listen to their words, for what a man speaks comes from the bottom of his heart. We are all different trees bearing different fruits. We can be mixed together in the same bowl but we will remain unique in taste and character. Some are sour while some are bitter. Others are sweet while others are hard like nuts. We are different like various fruits in the same bowl.

If you taste a fruit you can be able to describe the tree that the fruit was picked from. Trees produce after their kind. Apple trees produce apples while peach trees produce peaches. Each apple will have seeds in it that will produce another generation of apple trees. Some trees are good while others are bad but all of them will reproduce after their kind. We can always identify a tree by its fruit. Even Jesus confirms it in the book of Matthew when he says, "You shall know the tree by its fruits." There is an important lesson here for all of us. We need to protect our hearts from poisonous seeds so we can produce good fruit.

The Poisonous Trees

Poisonous trees bear poisonous fruit. They can fall into the following catergories:

- Trees whose fruit makes you lazy
- Trees whose fruit makes you jealous
- Trees whose fruit makes you fearful
- Trees whose fruit makes you feel condemned
- Trees whose fruit makes you become proud
- Trees whose fruit makes you become stingy

Those trees can be anyone who is around you. It can be someone you trust, someone you visit or even someone you live with in the same house. It can be leaders of the community, people at your workplace people you love. They can make you fruitful or poison you.

People who are close to your heart have an undeniable power to influence your life for good or for evil. Businessmen mostly give birth to entrepreneurs. Pastors give birth to spiritual sons and daughters. If you find someone who suffers with anxiety or mediocrity don't look further than his surroundings or his leaders for the cause. He is like that because of the people he is surrounding himself with or eats from.

If you surround yourself with working people you will be employed. If you walk with business people you will be a businessman. In the same way most spiritual sons become what their spiritual fathers are. If you are an evangelist you have the potential to give birth to a lot of evangelists like you. If you are a pastor you also have the potential to give birth to a lot of pastors. People become what they always listen to and observe and mostly reflect their environment. If you are wet it shows that you are coming from the rain. If you are jealous and always complaining it shows that you lack progress and you don't have potential to produce fruit or to prosper.

Every aspect of our character is a reflection of the seed that we have allowed to be planted in our hearts. This is why I have chosen to read books and to watch DVDs and go to church. If you feed yourself with wisdom you will grow in wisdom and become wise. If you feed yourself with corruption you will surely be corrupt. I must know you by the fruit you bear. I can see you through your congregation or through your employees.

Be Yourself

God expects you to be excellent in what you do by being you and not by imitating someone else. He has made you unique and given you your own path to walk. I get inspired by many things on television - especially by the Paralympics. I marvel as I watch disabled people expressing themselves and excelling in what they are doing. In athletics some run without legs - making use of running blades.

I see people using their feet to write books because they don't have hands. Others have speech impediments and yet are motivational speakers. I am writing this to show you that you too can bear fruits just as you are regardless of your limitations. Start to realise that you are unstoppable with God on your side. You are above all odds. Search yourself and discover what you are good at. It doesn't matter what your weaknesses are. All of us have our own weaknesses but we don't want to focus on them. Let us instead focus on excelling and becoming fruitful in what we do.

You can't be a tree that bears all kind of fruits. You have to become a specialist - a master of your own flavour. No one can compete with you. If I don't have a voice to sing it doesn't mean I can't preach. We are the different flavours in one big bowl. If I don't have legs it doesn't mean that I can't study or I can't become a fashion designer. I am a miracle myself. I'm not a failure. I'm good in my own way. I can write books and sing new songs. I can sell apples and make things happen.

I can be fruitful and bear any good fruits in God's provision. So can you. I'm a talented tree with potential to bear fruit in every area of my life. I make things happen not by my power but by the power of the Holy Spirit and through the grace of God. I have Christ in me and that is why I bear fruit. I will not allow bad seed to be planted in my soil but will give an ear to the people who provoke greatness in me.

You shall know me through what I do or say. If I speak good things in your ears I'll make you grow and be free. If I speak fear and condemnation, I will kill the good seed in you. When I took a closer look I realized that Christ preached the good news because He wanted to draw out the goodness in us so that we could bear good fruit.

Don't judge me by my appearance but by what I do and by what I'm still going to do. Judge me by the fruit I produce. It is through my fruit that you can know my thoughts and intentions. If I produce good fruit, I am good. You shall know what kind of tree I am by examining my fruit. Fruits always represent the tree that produced them. I represent my heavenly Father. One way or another you will notice who my Master and Pillar is. My excellence points to my Master and Lord of my spirit.

Musa Mobongwa

Introducing Your Fruit in a Fruitful Manner

One day I was in Roodepoort Library doing some research. I was on the internet for almost three hours when I started to feel the need to take a break. My mind was just exhausted. When I stepped out to rest I met a man who was on his smoking break. It was our first meeting but we were soon conversating as if we'd known each other for a very long time. He had gone for an interview in a certain company in Sandton that had a vacancy for one call centre employee. I was eager to hear more because he was so friendly and positive. There was only one vacancy and he started to lose hope when he noticed the large number of people standing in the queue. I was intrigued by his tale. He was hoping to get the job but the fact that he had forgotten his CV at his place made him feel discouraged.

I put my hands in my pockets and looked him straight in the eye. "I don't know what was going on in my head for me to forget my CV," he said. I looked at him differently when he said that and it led me to ask him how he could have forgotten his CV at home when going for an interview. He tossed his cigarette butt in the smokers' bin and said that he sometimes thought he would get the opportunity to email it through after his interview. My mind started to preach for me. It convinced me that this man was not prepared and didn't do his research thoroughly. My mind further convinced me that this man was not serious about finding a job. If he could think like

48

that, just imagine what was going through his interviewer's mind.

Every tree introduces itself by the flavor of its fruits. Just imagine what the interviewer thought about this guy. Maybe they concluded that he would also forget their files everywhere. They might have also concluded that he was not serious about their interview and, by implication, not serious about the job either. It was obvious that he was not prepared. Employers always fill their vacancies with people who are prepared.

Preparing Thoroughly

As I pondered on how unprepared this man was, my mind drifted to my mother. When she is preparing to make her home-cooked jam she picks the ripe and ready peaches or apricots and leaves the raw and rotten ones on the tree. She doesn't pick the raw ones and leave the ripe ones. She also doesn't pick pears or apples when she wants to make apricot jam. Your preparations have to align with what you want to produce. I can't go for a presentation to report on the status of a project without taking the necessary documentation with me. I must have done my research and collected all necessary information, dress appropriately and use proper language. By preparing adequately I will feel confident. That will increase my faith. Did you know that people judge you based on how you present yourself.

The book of Matthew 7:17 says, " Likewise, every good tree bears good fruit, but a bad tree bears bad fruit.". That is true. Good people do good works. They share the good news, empower, uplift, motivate, and comfort others. I'm not saying you must go around giving people money. Indeed we all need money but that is not what it's about. We were called to preach the good news and to build each other up in Christ. Tell them it's possible and show them the way without judging them. Help them to bear good fruit.

Be Deeply Rooted in Christ

We will know you by your fruit and the words you speak which are the fruit of your lips. Christians who are deeply rooted in Christ have this in common - they bear good fruit and pray without ceasing. My friend Solly told me that when he started to work in the retail industry he didn't know anyone. After three months he had a lot of 'born again' friends. He started to grow spiritually but, if I may ask, how did he know them? He used the gift of discernment to identify those of like spirit. We are not the same as the children of the world and sometimes they can't handle us. When I speak, the non-spiritual people often say I'm a liar while I know exactly what I'm talking about. If you are rooted in Christ your spirit is always preaching and praying and the Holy Spirit always shows you the hidden things of God. If you are really rooted in Christ your words become life giving. It's not easy to hide yourself when you're rooted in Christ because the fruit comes forth by itself. Whatever you speak doesn't come from your mind but from Jesus in you.

I was working the night shift one day with several other people when one of the guys started talking very negatively about his life. I tried to ignore it but the Spirit in me convicted me so harshly that I had to burst out of my bubble. I said, "Stop what you are saying about your life because you will cause your life to be worse and worse. Don't you know that the power of life and death is in your tongue?" I looked at him with compassion. He didn't even know that I was born again but he immediately asked me if I was a born again Christian. I didn't answer him.

That's what I'm talking about. The Spirit will push you to utter the words from God even when you don't want to talk. God will surely force you to utter His word as a solution. If someone around you is sick, hopeless or vulnerable, the Spirit of God will push you until you help. If you resist Him you will feel guilty. That's what happens to someone who is rooted in Jesus Christ. You give forth His fruits first above your will because Christ is now living in you.

A man was preaching in a train I was in once and I heard him say these words, "I saw someone who was ill last week in town. The Holy Spirit told me to pray for him but I didn't obey. I felt so guilty after that. I was sure that if I had obeyed the voice of the Holy Spirit that person was going to be healed." That's what happens when you disobey the Holy Spirit. You will feel like you lost something in your life. You need to pray for the strength to obey the One who dwells in you.

Everyone who is rooted in Him will do the will of the Father so that they can bear fruit in Christ according to the seed He has planted in you. Don't be full of yourself. You must be full of the One who is in control of your life so that His fruits can spring forth for the benefit of those around you.

Chapter Four
Resurrecting The Dead Fruit

Do you believe in resurrection? My answer to that is, "Yes I do and I believe you do too." I also believe that Jesus died and resurrected after three days. Because he resurrected we can also resurrect in our health, our businesses and our careers. You can regain anything you've lost in your life - your dreams, your health and even your marriage. Some people have lost so much that they think all hope is gone. They don't even want to try anything anymore because of past disappointments. We have to realise that when Jesus is our master resurrection power becomes accessible to us.

Jesus describes Himself as the true vine, us as the branches, and our Father in Heaven as the master who takes care of Him. We all know that Jesus died and he resurrected again after three days. The Bible tells us that he resurrected with power. We all know that the power of resurrection belongs to God. It is written in 1 Corinthians

6:14 that "By His power God raised the Lord from the dead and He will also raise us."

If your seed is dead, it doesn't mean that God can't resurrect it. It might look like it is sealed in a tomb as Jesus was but it doesn't mean that the power of God can't resurrect it. Don't look for more than the power of God. Through His Word He can resurrect your dead situations and even your dying career. Don't look for more than the Word of God because He is able to raise your dead seed from the tomb. He will cause it to live and bear fruit. He can resurrect any dead dream and any situation.

You are a branch drawing life from Him. If He dies you die and if He resurrects you also resurrect. I used to watch my grandfather when he was helping us to prune trees back at home. He would put on his gloves to protect his hands from scratches then take the wooden saw and step ladder. He would cut down all the dead, dry branches and leave the good, fruitful ones. After he was done he would give me the dry branches to use as firewood the coming winter.

He once taught me that if you cut down the dry and fruitless branches, you are helping the remaining ones to be more fruitful. After pruning he would spray the trees with a poison to kill all the pests which destroy the fruits. When harvest time came our trees would bear huge, beautiful and healthy fruits.

This is what God does in our lives when He is preparing us for resurrection. He cuts off all the bad and dry branches that kill your potential and leaves the good and fruitful ones that will prosper you. He knows that if He leaves the bad branches in your life, they will end up affecting the good ones. His strategy is to cut off all the bad branches then water and prune the fruitful ones so that they can become more and more fruitful.

Every dead situation testifies to the fact that it was once alive. When someone with resurrection power comes along they will unleash new life to the dry bones. Lazarus was dead but his body was still there as evidence that he had been alive. Jesus came to Lazarus' tomb more than three days after his death when his flesh was already decomposing. Yes, his flesh was rotting and smelling but all Jesus needed were his bones to bring him back to life. He didn't focus on the smelly and rotten body but on Lazarus' potential to live again. It is the same when it comes to your life. He cuts off the bad branches so that your full potential can be realized.

I am here to tell you that Jesus wants to resurrect your dead dreams. If you can show Him the evidence that you were once dreaming to be this or that, He will take it from there. Just look for the evidence in your storeroom or in your office. Look for that contract you thought you had no chance of getting. Look for your marriage certificate or your matric certificate. Show Him the evidence, pray and fast. Start afresh. Speak to Him about it, confess it, and resurrect it in your heart. Consider it an opportunity to prove your faith in Him. Trust in Him and your dream will stand up even if it was dead. If you believe, everything is possible and all grace and several chances belong to Him. It's time to let Him take away your fears, your doubts, your unforgiving heart, and prideful attitudes. Seek Him for help with your heart and let Him work on you.

Sometimes in life I would think that I was wasting my time with whatever I was trying to do because it was not working out. I assumed that I must be busy with something I wasn't good at. Many of us may have given up on what we wanted to be or on what we wanted to achieve because of our mind-set. We settled for much less because of rejection, manipulation, disappointment, discourageement, and mockery.

We walk around with a defeated mindset, believing everything that negative people have been saying about us. The truth though is that all of those negative words that have been spoken over our lives are lies. God is not moved by them and if you take even a small piece of dead bone to Him and ask for restoration and resurrection, He can turn your situation around. Obey Him when He tells you what to do about your life and run with it. Dream big and speak life to it. Keep confessing what you want for your life.

Why do you focus on what people said to you or about you? They might have sown bad seeds in you but you are also carrying good seeds in your heart. You might be a tree with both good and bad branches but if you set your mind on the dry branches you will die slowly and become dry. It's time to turn your mind to the fruitful branches so that you can bear more good fruit. It doesn't mean that the dry branches won't get hold of you sometimes, but you must allow your God to break them off and throw them into the fire. Let Him continue pruning the fruitful ones so that you can excel in bearing more fruit and resurrect what was dead.

Don't allow disappointments to dwell in your heart and go around carrying them in your spirit. Only allow good things to take root in your spirit. If you focus on the good things you have – no matter how small - and appreciate them, the Lord will resurrect them even if you thought they were already dead.

Why You Need Resurrection

We read a very interesting account in the Bible about a woman named Dorcas. The name Dorcas is a Greek translation of the Aramaic name Tabitha. She was a very good disciple and served the community well but sadly, she fell ill and died. When we read further we find that the other disciples were very hurt by her death and were in deep sorrow because of their loss. Just imagine what it would be like if your own community lost someone who was full of good works.... It shows me that if you have a gift you cannot leave it dead because your gift is your Tabitha in your community. Tabitha was a good gift to the community and so is your gift.

When the disciples heard that Peter was in their community, they sent two disciples to tell him that Tabitha was dead in the hope that he would come quicker. I hope you feel that way about your dead dream where you just can't wait for someone to restore it. Peter came at last and the Bible tells us that when he arrived, he was taken to the sickroom where Tabitha's body had been laid. Her body was the evidence that she was once alive. Peter prayed, took her by the hand and she rose up from the dead!

You Need Someone to Raise Your Tabitha

My goal in writing this chapter about the power of resurrection is to let you know why you need your Tabitha to be resurrected. Are you really feeling pain for your lost dream and vision? Are your dead visions good for the community? If they are you have every right to call on the Lord for help. Ask Him in Jesus name to raise your Tabitha from the dead.

God will restore your vision and bring it to life again. He will water the soil of your heart and destroy all the worms, birds and locusts that are damaging your fruits but He will only do this if is for a good cause like Tabitha. Learn to bless other people with your gift. Heal someone, give to someone in need, uplift the fallen, or motivate someone. Don't let your dream to make music, act, preach, or write die. Call on Jesus to lift it up. Don't be comfortable watching your gift going into the tomb but look for someone to help you attend some seminars. Go to church. Buy some good books. Pray, fast and hold on.

Let Him resurrect your seed and bring it to life. Maybe your Tabitha will come with healing for the sick again or come with new hope for your community again. Maybe your Tabitha will bring a smile to single parents again. Maybe your Tabitha will give orphans hope again. Maybe your Tabitha will build the church again. Maybe your Tabitha will take your country foward again. What I'm saying is this, "Let your Tabitha be for the good work of the Lord." God will resurrect your Tabitha and cause you to testify about His resurrection power just as the disciples did who were so desperate for Tabitha's life to be restored. You will prosper everywhere you go when your dreams are not about you but are about helping the next person.

You must complete God's will and purpose in the world. Give to the needy. Pray for people and sing a new song to them. Write books for the people and preach the good news to them. Give people jobs so that they can provide for their families. Be the change - the miracle. Be like the disciples who resurrected Tabitha for a good cause. You are the tree that God is relying on to bear fruit in the world. That is why He is resurrecting your fruit or dreams today. You can't just forget about your purpose. Go out there and fight the good fight of faith. Work hard under His anointing so that He can heal your pain and lighten your burden. He won't let you down.

He Supplies in Our Dead Situations

If you are sick the fruit you need is healing. If you are poor it is riches and if you are spiritually empty you need to be spiritually filled. If you are a dry branch you have to be restored and made green. We have weaknesses that oppose our strengths so we must let our strengths rise above our weaknesses because we must be fruitful. It is our portion to be strong. The Bible says, "Let the weak say I'm strong. Let the poor say I'm rich. Let the sick say I'm healed." We are planted to be fruitful. If we are submitted to the Lord's will for our lives, His plans for us will manifest in us.

God's Reasons to Resurrect

In the thirty-seventh chapter of the book of Ezekiel from the third verse, the Bible speaks about the dry bones in the valley. Prophet Ezekiel was being trusted to bring about the resurrection of the dry bones that God had a purpose for. It might have been Prophet Ezekiel who spoke over the bones but it was the God of resurrection who brought them to life. The Bible says that after Ezekiel prophesied the bones became alive and became a great army. God's mission is to make a great army out of your dead and dry branches. Your dreams might look like they belong in a bygone era but God wants you to speak life over them so that they can become alive and be a great army for His purposes. You are the one who must speak over them. They will hear the word of God through you, come alive and run with the mission of God.

If you have given up your music dream, it's time to speak the word of prophecy over it so that it becomes alive. Do you know that your gift can heal the world and that the whole world is desperate for what you have? Now is the time to make yourself available for God's purpose. Pray over your dream and plant a seed for your dream so that it can take root again. God wants to restore your dead branches so that they are renewed to bear fruit. Now is the time to sacrifice your time, your money, and your spirit to God and start to live your dream in Him again. All things are possible to those who trust in the Lord. Our mission is to restore our fruitfulness through Jesus Christ.

You might have lost your father, your mother, your sister, or your wife. Maybe something is wrong with your health. Whatever it is, God is still there with you. Even if you have lost everything, God can still restore your life. Job lost everything - his belongings, his sons and daughters, his business, his houses, and even the respect of his wife too. He lost his health and his body was covered in painful boils. Because of his faith, everything that he lost was restored back to him. If God can do it for Job He can still do it for you. Keep your faith in God and prophesy over your dead situation till restoration comes. Be the fruitful tree and never lose faith in the word of God.

Fight the good fight of faith. The same power that restored the dry bones in the valley is the same power that restored all that Job lost. It is the same power that restored Jesus from the dead and Tabitha can also testify about this resurrection power. We don't walk by sight but by faith. We have the power to take back what the enemy has stolen from us. If we can pray and trust God, our lives will never be the same again. We can continue bearing fruit more and more and our God is able to restore a double portion of all that we have lost.

When I was growing up one of my friends had a rich father. He dressed well and had an expensive phone. He was the only one with that kind of phone. One day it was stolen in school and he reported the theft to the class teacher. The teacher insisted on searching every class but the phone was not found. My friend called his father and explained what had happened. His father just said, "Don't worry. I'll buy you another one." After three months he had a new phone - better than the one which was stolen.

This is the same thing that our God does. God is the richest father imaginable and He can replace all of your stolen goods because He loves you with a father's love. He cares about you physically, mentally, financially, and spiritually. He will go an extra mile to resurrect whatever has been taken from you. He does it so that you can be happy. Your joy is His concern so tell Him what you have lost and what you want back. Pray to Him. Prophesy over that area of your life. His plan for you is to restore you and make you fruitful.

Chapter Five
Spiritual Fruit

I didn't know about spiritual fruits until I became a born again Christian. The Holy Spirit also taught me the importance of putting them into practice. These spiritual fruits are love, joy, peace goodness, gentleness, longsuffering and faith. They operate in our lives while we are waiting for the glory of God to be revealed in our lives. They are the fruits that are given to someone who is walking in accordance with the Holy Spirit of God. They are the key to success in all areas of our lives. If you put them into practice you will unlock promotion and healing in every area of your life. They unleash the power of God to minister supernaturally to those who walk with Him.

Whoever bears these spiritual fruits shall prosper everywhere he goes and in everything he touches. He will be a success. Let me remind you about Joseph who was sold by his brothers to the Ishmaelites for 20 silver coins. The bible says he was having dreams about being a king over his brothers, his father and his mother. His brothers became jealous after they heard the interpretation of

Joseph's dream that their father Jacob gave. So extreme was their jealousy that they conspired to kill him.

My own life is also similar to that of Joseph. People would hate me because of my dreams. I know some of you reading this book have been fired from their jobs, some have lost friends and others were laughed at. If you have endured this kind of persecution you must know that it's the jealousy in them that makes them feel like you are better than them. Situations like this show me clearly that dreamers are threats to people who don't have a vision for their own future. When we read on we see that Joseph's brothers were not fighting against him but against his dreams. That's why they didn't call him by his name Joseph anymore. They started to call him by the name Dreamer which was a sign that Joseph's dreams were bothering them.

If you have a dream and favour from God, no one can stop you. The Lord will cause people to see something special in you. You will display these spiritual fruits and people will feel free and empowered when they are next to you. People will be drawn to you and want to support you. The Bible says you shall know the tree by its fruits.

Joseph was sold by his brothers to the Ishmaelites so that he would never taste his dream of becoming a king. His brothers' mission was to kill him before he could taste his future. They didn't know that the vision was not in their hands or within their control but in the dreamer's spirit and heart. It is only God who can plant dreams in the hearts of dreamers and it is only God who can stop the dream from coming to pass. If you sell the dreamer you sell the dream also. The seed is in the dreamer's heart so they will exercise their dreams everywhere and anywhere they are. It doesn't matter how difficult the situation you throw them in is, they can still exercise their leadership skills in a foreign country or in jail as long as the seed of the dream is in them.

They shall give birth to spiritual fruit like Joseph did. If the enemies of the dream sell him, the buyer will buy him and the dream in him. No one can separate what God has put together. If he was dreaming of becoming a king in his own land, he can still dream of becoming a king in the foreign land. If he doesn't give up he will still live his dream because God-given dreams are meant to come true for anyone who exercises these spiritual fruits. These dreams never die as long as you don't give up. Joseph never gave up so don't give up. Fight the good fight of faith. It doesn't matter where you are, what you have or don't have. It doesn't matter how much you earn. The dream itself will pave a way.

If you have dreams you will always be fighting demons and negative energy from people who are against you just as Joseph did. Their agenda is to interrupt your future but it doesn't mean that you can't realise your dreams anymore. If you exercise the spiritual fruit every day of your life surely you shall prosper in everything you touch. Joseph's Egyptian master saw that Joseph was prosperous in everything he did. He bore much fruit because God was with him.

I was not there in Joseph's times but based on my research I can tell you that it wasn't easy for Joseph to be in that foreign country. His attitude made the environment better for him though. Maybe other slaves were envying him because his master favoured him more than others. I'm sure that he was gentle to everyone around him and he was a seeker of peace. He didn't complain when given difficult or unpleasant tasks but worked willingly in spite of being a slave in Egypt. In the midst of this challenging situation he didn't give up or lose track of his dream. He waited patiently for the Lord in a foreign land. He still waited in faith for the promise of God. Inside he was a king over the nations even while he was seen as a slave on the outside. Joseph chose to focus on what was inside rather than on the outward reality.

People with spiritual fruit go through a lot of persecution without seeking revenge and God blesses them without limitations. They don't pay back evil for evil deeds perpetrated against them but they bless those who curse them. They do their best even in their suffering, when circumstances are uncomfortable. They still bear good fruit. The Bible says that Egypt prospered because of Joseph's blessings. Can you imagine your country being saved because of your slavery? He saved Egypt from the famine. Egypt had masters and leaders but none of them saw it coming. God chose to reveal Himself through a slave.

That's the power of spiritual fruit. God lifted him up and made him share the inheritance of citizens. I can see evidence of the fruit of the spirit in Joseph. He forgave his brothers who sold him to the Egyptians without seeking revenge. He gave his brothers food during the famine. God will take you to a broken country to be His solution. He can make you a president in a foreign land to be the solution for those who have oppressed you.

Joseph suffered for a long time - being thrown into the pit, accused of rape, and thrown into jail - but the Bible calls him a blessed man who carried out the will of God. It is the same for me and you. You might have been fired for no reason, retrenched, or even imprisoned for crimes you didn't commit, but to God you are still blessed.

Practise forgiveness not for them but for you. We go through painful things in life but we know that we must produce long-suffering, love, kindness, faith, passion, goodness and peace everyday. These spiritual fruits are our weapons for everyday battles. We must operate in spiritual fruits till we get the wisdom and understanding stored up in them. When we endure trials we bear good fruit in Jesus Christ that makes us conquer storms. We sow seed that will make us bear fruits that will cause us to inherit businesses we didn't build, to occupy positions we didn't study for, and to get healing from diseases that have no cure.

We will be like the slaves who eat the inheritance of sons because of the spiritual fruit we are bearing. We are sons and daughters of God. We are the heads and not the tails. We are the chosen generation - the glory of God. Jesus is the true vine and we are the branches that draw life from him so we are fruitful.

In 2012 I was attending church in an area of Roodepoort called Princess. I remember one beautiful Sunday when the Spirit of the Lord was moving in the church in spite of the extreme heat. When testimony time came, people stood up and came forward to testify about what the Lord has done for them in challenging circumstances. I saw the hand of God when a sister named Amanda shared her testimony. I wish you could have been there to hear it for yourself.

Amanda told us how she had received a big house for free. She said, "My mother and I were dreaming about building a house in our home area for so many years. Things didn't go according to plan so it seemed like we'd never build that house. The situations and troubles we were facing tempted us to give up on our dream but glory be to Jesus!" She was pacing up and down the stage in her high heels with the microphone in hand with the joy of the Lord all over her face. The glory of God was all over her as she continued her testimony. "My mother worked for her bosses for fifteen years as a domestic worker," she said. "We could not afford the house with the salary my mother was earning but glory to Jesus!"

Everyone in the church was captivated by her testimony and was itching to hear more. "Suddenly my mother's bosses just decided to relocate to America. Our immediate worry was that once they left there would be no more salary. Even if the salary couldn't get us a house, it was better than nothing." I was filled with compassion for them as I considered their predicament.

Amanda continued saying, "One day they took us out for dinner for the very first time at a very expensive restaurant in town. I was wondering what was going on with these people to do this after so many years? While I was asking myself these questions the boss's husband said, 'Thank you for all of the years you have worked for us - for your kindness, love, and peace even when we scolded you for no reason. We were like a family.' My mother and I were looking at each other in surprise wondering what was going on when the boss's wife smiled and took a document from her handbag and gave it to us to read. 'You were faithful to us for so many years," she began, "now my husband and I have decided to give you our house as a token of our gratitude for everything you have done for us.'"

The congregation erupted in praise because of what we had just heard. Amanda said, "I'm telling you my brothers and sisters in Christ, my mom and I didn't see it coming. God provided the house just like that after a long time of suffering. They were so hard on my mom over the years that I never thought they noticed my mother's kindness."

God knows you more than you know yourself. He sees all the good works you are doing. Even if your earthly master behaves like they do not see anything - God sees all the good works you are doing. He will reward you according to the fruits you are bearing. Whatever you sow in the spirit you don't sow in vain but you will reap fruit when the time is right. God is busy preparing your harvest and He can never disappoint you.

Don't give up. In everything you do, remain in the peace and joy of Him who is working a good work in you. It shall come to pass. His promises are yes and amen. The Bible says that the words of God shall not return to Him void. This means you are on the right track. Do whatever God is placing on your heart – the things you love that bring you joy. Do good to everyone and don't be afraid to be like God in the flesh. The Bible says that Jesus considered it not robbery to be equal to God.

Avoid Fear

Fear destroys the fruit of the spirit. It is the devil's weapon to make you hopeless and to give up. You must remember that all that comes from fear is sin and sin kills. This means that fear kills. We were not given the spirit of fear but of love and power. We have access to power from above to help us conquer fear. That power is the Word of God. The Word of God is there to build up our faith and help us to be spiritual so that we can bear the fruits of the spirit. If you are a 'born again' Christian it is your portion to bear fruit. The Spirit of God is fruitful and whosoever walks in the spirit must bear the fruits of the spirit. Renew your mind with the Word of God. Know the will of God for your life because His will is the future He wants for you. Through Him we excel. We go beyond limitations because His Word enables us to not give up. He renews our strength every morning.

He gives us hope in dry situations and makes us see things differently. People get surprised and ask me questions because sometimes they see me enjoying myself in hard situations. I always ask them, "Why must I complain or cry about the situation?" That attitude makes me look mindless but I walk by faith and not by sight. I speak the Word of God through all my pain.

My elder brother once asked me why I don't speak about my problems. I didn't answer him aloud but the answer in my heart was that I can't speak about my problems to people because they have the ability to make a small problem look huge. I go to God with my problems. People will get you into fear and you will become so afraid that you will be unable to do anything about your situation. We lose the battles of life because our fears cause us to believe the lie that the enemy is more powerful than we are. The truth is that God gave us power to overcome the enemy and fully armed us with mighty weapons for the battle.

Musa Mobongwa

Chapter Six

The Fruits Of Giving

I believe in giving. Giving is very spiritual and very fruitful to those who believe and act on it. Did you know that you can change the lives of a million people by giving one person a good gift? I didn't say 'by giving a lot of money' but 'by giving a good gift' which is acceptable to God. Giving is very powerful. It's not only pastors and doctors who can heal; givers of good gifts can heal too! Giving is from the heart and can make a great impact in people's lives. It can open the future and create everlasting joy for generations to come. Giving is always going an extra mile. It is a powerful weapon against the devil. It is not just about giving money, but also motivation, advice, love, and so on.

Some of us go to church where we sit down to listen to the Word of God. The Word of God is what transforms us to be what God wants us to be. In church we are empowered and healed, we receive miracles and deliverance from the hand of the enemy. We get hope and learn to walk in abundant life. We receive so much but do we give in return? Do you think the church could stand without giving money, love, hope, motivation, and prayers? The foundation of the church is Jesus whom the world received as a gift from God the Father. We are given so that we can give. We are forgiven but can only receive it when we forgive others in return. That is why Jesus said, "Give and you shall be given." Giving is the foundation of all the good gifts.

When You Give You Plant a Seed

We plant seeds sometimes that grow to be far bigger than our natural eyes can see or comprehend. We want to see the results of our giving for our own sakes but to God it's not about us but about His kingdom. There was a woman of God who sowed money into the offering basket every Sunday. She would tell me that she felt like God wasn't accepting her gift. She couldn't understand why she was giving faithfully while receiving nothing from God. I said to her, "Giving is not selfish. When you speak like that, it sounds selfish. Even if you haven't received anything you are praying for yet, you are still going to receive it. We, the church appreciate your gift because we need food in the storehouse. I said, "Look around you. People are happy and a lot of good things are happening. Testimonies are being told. That's the power of your gift so thank God that you are part of the miracles happening in the church. It's not about you all the time but about the body of Christ". I told her, "If you want to see the power of your gift manifesting in church, invite someone to church." She invited someone new and that person got born again. The Bible says that Heaven rejoices when one sinner repents.

There is a miracle in that basket. When you give you're simply saying that the Gospel must go forth and be fruitful and people must be healed. People grow spiritually and many get eternal life in heaven just because of your gift. The Gospel won't go anywhere without givers in the church. Giving is a powerful ministry in itself. Tithing, offering, pledges, and first fruits are all important to take the work of the Kingdom foward. Jesus told His disciples, "Go all over the world and preach the gospel." We must know that no one can go all over the world without petrol, clothes and food. Nowadays all of these things need money. Let the work of the Lord be your concern.

We give to God and He gives to us. We are coworkers with Him in saving the world. When we give to God, it's the same as giving to ourselves because the same kingdom we are building is going to make us and our children fruitful. It's going to make us prosper every-where we go. I was not going to be where I am today if it was not for the preachers and givers in the Kingdom of God. If you see me standing or yourself walking in faith you must know that someone gave. We all receive when we hear the Word of God.

Faith comes by hearing the Word of God. You heard the Word from the shepherd you are following and you give him the honour that he deserves as a man of God. We might not hear anything about the people who are building the Kingdom by giving gifts of money and prayers. The glory must be to God who teaches us to give so that the preachers can continue to build us up in our faith. We live and walk by faith and not by sight. Don't undermine your gift. Your giving is eventually going to change someone's life and touch generations still to come. By giving you build a legacy in the kingdom of God.

You are a tree that bears a lot of different kinds of fruit. Some will surprise you because you didn't know that your gift had the capacity to produce them. Some you will never taste because they were not for you but a blessing for others. God will continue to give you whatever you ask in Jesus' name because of your good heart and in accordance with the knowledge you have received from the men and women of God who have ministered the gospel to you.

These days we can receive the Word of God wherever we are. We listen to it in our cars, on our cell phones, radios, and in our homes on television. This is possible because people are giving and planting the seed for us so that we don't have to wait for Sunday to hear the Word. It's all about the seed planted in us that will give forth fruit. The Word is a seed planted in you and it shall not return to God void.

God said, "Test me in tithes and offerings and see if I will not open the windows of heaven for you." When you give tithes, give them to the house where your soul is fed.

Many children of God tithe without experiencing an open Heaven because there is no food in the house. You have to give tithes to the Lord so that your shepherd can open the floodgates of heaven for you by giving you a fruitful word from Heaven. When a shepherd releases a word that is not from God it holds the people back from their blessings and a perverted word can even destroy innocent people. God preserved the scriptures for us so that we could be fruitful. He wanted to make sure that we would have good food in His house, which is the Word of God.

Tithe so that there can be food in the house of the Lord. This scripture places a lot of responsibility upon pastors. God is trusting the preachers to unlock the gates of Heaven for the people through the pure and powerful Word of God when they give of their tithes. The Word is that seed sown by the Son of Man spoken of in Matthew 13:37. It causes the tither to bear fruit and testify. God only answers His own Word which He has elevated above all of His Names.

It Always Feels Good to Give

One day I was holding my "mageu" in my hand while waiting for the train to come in at Florida station in Roodepoort. I watched as more and more people came into the waiting room. Suddenly I heard people screaming from nowhere. I got a little frightened and rushed to find out what was happening. A woman had fainted and was laying on the ground. We helped her up and asked her what was wrong but she didn't say a single word.

One guy asked her where she was coming from and she said she was from the clinic. We asked her if she had eaten anything and her answer was, "No." Another guy, putting two and two together, concluded, "This woman is dizzy from an injection. This is an after effect of the medicine taken on an empty stomach." On hearing this I offered her the mageu that I had bought for myself so that she could drink it and gain strength. She drank it and felt much better afterwards. I felt like I had done something huge for her. It always feels good to help. If giving away such a small thing like mageu can make you feel like you're on top of the world, imagine how fulfilling it is to give away big things to people in need of our help.

When you give God rejoices in Heaven and speaks of you with pride as He spoke of Job's righteousness. When you give He will make sure that you always have so that you can continue to do His will. Giving will make you feel good and God will just keep multiplying what you have. Giving makes people feel like heroes. Giving in the church is so fulfilling that it makes you want to give even more. When you feel good after giving, know that your gift has moved God.

There Are Different Types of Gifts

There was a lady who was broken after her fiancé cheated on her and dumped her. She started to ask herself a lot of questions. She started to think that she was not beautiful and it made her feel insecure. One day she happened to tune in to a radio program when a motivational speaker was addressing the problems we face in life. She received hope and started to feel good about herself again. She even took notes to read later. Money is not the only thing we can give. We can give motivation, love, comfort, time, and advice. Give of what you have. Visit the rejected.

I remember one day I visited a friend, only to find that he was very stressed and depressed. He was so happy to see me that he told me everything that was bothering him. I just motivated him and told him what was possible through Jesus Christ. He was so happy and thanked me. I saw his smile coming back as he received supernatural healing of his emotions. I was happy for him and felt like a hero too. I was on top of the world. As people we take such things for granted but to God it is really big. To God you are a hero indeed.

Planting a Financial Seed

I was always asking myself why I had to tithe and keep giving or sowing financial seeds. I was always asking why until God said to me, "You want to reap financial fruit but you never plant any seed?" God said, "Plant the seed, take care of it and don't let it die." From that I have learned to carry on taking care of what I had just planted. Plant financial seed so that your financial life can be fruitful. The money you have is not too little for you to give. Most of the time the real problem is a stingy spirit. We are meant to be fruitful in every area of our lives.

Musa Mobongwa

Give the Best of Your Talent to the World

Give your all and inspire people through your talent. When you excel in your talent you give those around you hope. In the year 2000 there was a dance group by the name of Masutsa Dance Crew. The first time I saw them was in Phuthaditjhaba. I was so inspired as I sat there watching them dance. They danced skillfully and their moves were poetic. They made it look so effortless that I even thought I could do it too. One of them would speak poetically while the others would interpret his words in dance. I was so motivated and felt like everything was possible. Masutsa Dance Crew gave it all and inspired the entire audience. I didn't join them but a lot of youth did. You must do your best to inspire your community and give people hope. I have been inspired by authors who give their best. Everyone who is doing their best is giving hope and inspiration to their country. I have seen people reaching for their dreams because they were inspired by their role models.

It's not a sin to look up to someone who blesses you or to look up to your role model. Pastors are always reading books and watching DVDs of other people who give their best. If you give your best, you can inspire someone to become something. You might even see people posting your pictures on walls because they see hope when they look at you. People are inspired by people who give their best. If you write a song, write a book or choreograph a dance routine - give your best. That talent is a gift that God gave you to give to others. The talent is a fruit itself.

My sister visited our aunt in Natal once and was so inspired by a delicious dish that my aunt cooked for her. Her heart started to burn with a desire to learn to cook like my aunt. When she came back all she could talk about was cooking and she was always busy experimenting in the kitchen. That is an example of how giving your best can transform the minds of those around us. If you give your best in what you cook you will trigger people's appetites. Some will even want your recipe. That is why athletes study their role model's life style. They want to know their fitness and dietary regime and even what kind of clothes they are wearing.

If you give your best to people they will always remember your good deeds. When you are gone the whole world will mourn for you. Giving your best always pays back. If you want to excel you must practise several times a day and push yourself beyond the limits. Always dream big and aim to break the record. If you believe it, you can be great as long as you take one step at a time. Every seed you plant is meant to germinate and grow. God is powerful enough to grant your request. Let achieving your vision fulfill you more than anything. If you want to give your best fruits to the world you will need to commit and sacrifice. Remember to cease every opportunity you have to give because you never know when you'll get another one. Always give your best.

Musa Mobongwa

Chapter Seven

The Fruitful Season

As dreamers and fruitful trees growing in God's will and purpose, we tend to forget that every fruit tree blossoms and bears fruit in its season. If you look at a peach tree in winter time you could be tempted to cut it down because of how dry it looks. It is the same with us humans. We often think of throwing in the towel when we go through dry seasons in our lives.

We tend to forget that we must wait for the right season. God has perfect timing. He is never too late or too early. He knows that if you bear too much fruit before your branches are strong enough some of your branches will break. He knows your capacity. When you ask God for something please make sure that you have enough room to receive it. You have to enlarge your territory before God can deliver your order. Make sure that you live a lifestyle of prayer and fasting to stay rooted in him. If you are not connected to him as a branch you will dry up and be thrown in the fire.

Every branch which is fruitful must know that four seasons must pass before it can bear fruit and be prepared to endure storms, hail, wind, and snow. What I'm saying is that you have to be strong and focus on your growth in Christ Jesus. A good example of this is my friend in the stationary business. He makes a good profit in the months of September through to January then the months from February through to August are very dry. Even in the good months challenges arise. I remember one time he had a client who refused to pay him till they ended up in court. Life is seasonal and when you blossom make sure you blossom for Christ.

I used to watch trees growing in the Free State and ask myself what it would be like to always be outside like a tree. Trees inspire me not to give up because in adverse environments they just keep growing taller and taller. When you see them in their glory it's easy to forget that they started out as small seeds. The tree grows through hard seasons. The rain falls on it and it still grows. August winds blow around it but the tree still grows. It grows through the cold of June and July looking forward to spring. It knows that spring is coming no matter what. You and I need to adopt that attitude. Know that whatever you face won't kill you but will make you focus more on your spring season when your fruits will manifest.

If a tree is focused on it's fruitful season what about you who is alive and rooted in Christ through the Spirit? You have all you need to fight and overcome your seasons. You are anointed to prevail as you push towards the mark of the high calling. When enemies rise against you, God shall raise the standard. All situations you are facing are there to make you strong and prepare you for tomorrow. We see your faith through your seasons.

If you are strong you must be prepared for the strongest of challenges. Even God Himself tests you according to your faith. We see your faith through the challenges you are overcoming. Your victories display your effort and potential. You and I are more than conquerors through Christ our Lord. We are the victors and our portion is always victory. All things work together for good for those who trust the Lord. People often think that they are unfruitful because of the dry season they are in and forget that seasons change. They need someone to remind them that they are still fruitful trees in the dry season. They just have to realise that their time is coming. Don't expect fruits at pruning time. The time to reap will come.

You Might be Tired From Waiting For So Long

We all feel tired and are sometimes tempted to complain. Complaining didn't start with us. Read the second chapter of Habakkuk and you'll understand what I'm speaking about. We see things one way and God sees them another way. Would you like it if everything went entirely your way without any challenges in your path? I wouldn't like that myself. I want some challenges so that I can get the victory through the Lord. How can my Father be proud of me if I don't defeat the opponent. Even when I fall several times in the battlefield, I'll still stand up and take the victory by fire or by force. Through Him I bear spiritual fruit within. Waiting for the Lord is good.

My God is omniscient and full of wisdom and with the love He has for me, He can never throw me in a fire that I cannot handle or give me sandals that I can't untie. When you have a child who is in school, I don't believe you would buy him a uniform that is too big for him. It won't fit and will be meaningless and useless to him. He will not be able to wear it to school. Buy him what is good and convenient for him. Another question I would ask is, "Can you buy your 8 year old child a house and say he must move out?" If we wouldn't do such an unreasonable thing why do we think that God would? He can never give you what is not right for you because it can end up endangering you.

My young brother once joined the Gym Company. He went only for a day and never went back again because he didn't observe proper training protocol. He had zeal to work out but made it difficult for himself then just decided to stop without letting us know what the problem was. `My young brother hurt himself by using weights that were too heavy for him because he wanted to gain muscle from one day of exercise. I asked him one day why he hadn't gone back to the gym when it was such a good initiative. He said his body had been painful for three days now since his workout. I just broke out in laughter till people were looking at us. I like to laugh and in my mind I was wondering what he had done wrong because I knew that he couldn't feel like that without a reason.

He didn't really want to talk about it but he came clean about what had happened. He said that he hadn't followed the instructor's instructions. My young brother was told not to use weights that were beyond his power because they would make his muscles sore. He was advised to start with small weights as a newcomer to the gym world. He was supposed to be patient and give his muscles time to develop the capacity to lift heavier weights. There is nothing wrong with starting small.

God doesn't want you to go down that path. He wants you to follow protocol without jumping stages. He knows somewhere somehow you will be disadvantaged because of the stage you didn't tackle. Teach yourself to walk step by step. Some people like short cuts too much and it sometimes backfires by sending them back to square one.

Wait for God's timing. Be patient until He is done pruning you. His time is the best time. He knows that if He gives you a car before you acquire a driver's license you will crash and face the consequences of your impatience. I doubt that any of us would be pleased to see their nine year old child driving a car to school without a driver's license. We must try by all means to avoid all the bad fruits of impatience. Progress is in us and we will move forward in due time. Greater is He that is in me than the one who is in the world. With progress in us we must not allow the one who is not progressive to destroy the future that God has for us.

God has good plans for your life. You must be fruitful and bear fruit patiently. Don't seek to enjoy fruit before time but wait for your season to reap. There's a time to work the soil, a time to plant the seed, a time for the tree to grow, a time to prune the tree, and a time to enjoy the fruit. The time is coming for you to be fruitful.

Preparing for the Good Times

In 2009 I was working in Middleburg in the province of Mpumalanga as a general worker. Sometimes I miss the people who were there with me because they were really good to me. I miss all the greenery and the sounds of different birds. It was just a peaceful land with a natural breeze. We were working at different departments and each morning I could station myself anywhere I wanted to as a general worker. One day in the month of August I was assisting the welder to join some broken kraal steel when I saw some of our drivers taking some big new tractors to the fields. As they drove past us the dust they raised changed the colour of the atmosphere. They were all heading straight to the farm to prepare the soil for the planting season.

Farmers don't make mistakes when they prepare for a harvest but work according to seasons and times. They always research the rainfall patterns and the makeup of the soil and apply the knowledge gained to benefit their farming. Everyone who is on a mission for God must prepare his field for the good season of sowing seed. Enlarge your hectares which represent your vision so that when the rain of God comes you will spring forth with power from the ground and grow till you bear fruits according to God's will.

Enlarge your mind and feed your spirit with the Word of God. When harvest time comes you will present yourself as a good tree to the Master. God doesn't use unprepared people. To be fruitful you must allow God to prepare you for the different seasons.

Don't Be Late and Don't Rush

What are we rushing for? People who rush often find themselves in massive debt with large housing loans and other credits. They fall prey to 'get rich quick' schemes and find themselves in depression as they sink into debt. God wants to transform your life so that you can be fruitful while others are owing far more than they can earn. After servicing their debts they are left with nothing in their bank accounts. You can approach debt counselors for help but you will still have to pay back what you owe.

That is not God's plan for us. He wants us to have faith and use our faith to acquire everything we need. If you want something that you do not have, save for it and wait patiently for the Lord. Why not create a second income? It's not a sign of greed to have seven incomes. Ask God for wisdom and obey His command. Follow His lead. Don't rely on your natural vision or make plans according to your natural understanding but operate in His will and His wisdom and wait patiently on His promises. Once you know that you have the promise, prepare your hectares.

There was a guy named Maduvha who studied to become a paramedic for three years because of his love for the profession. He and his friends struggled for many years to find work until he decided to think differently from them. He started to look for patterns so that he could identify the stronghold. He noticed that everywhere he tried to send his curriculum vitae he got the same response - they wanted people with experience. I like the way Maduvha transformed his mind. He didn't throw in the towel through all the disappointments but negotiated to be taken on as a volunteer so that he could gain the required experience.

After all he went through, his passion became fruitful for him. He can now work anywhere at anytime because of his good reputation and experience. He understood that he was supposed to prepare for his season so that when the rain fell he would be ready unlike before. Preparation will make you successful in everything you do. They say practice makes perfect and I have found it to be true. It makes people fruitful.

When you attempt something and are denied you are not left empty handed. You always gain information that will help you in the future. They will always tell you their requirements and give guidance if you seek it. If you are denied a job by the company of your dreams and told that you must first get a driver's license or get experience first – don't be discouraged. Let it motivate you to do what needs to be done and always say, "Thank you for the information." After that, make sure you do what you need to do to qualify. When you go back to them, they will eventually give you what you want. This law applies in the world of business as well. At times clients will tell you that they require a certain certificate or license that you do not have before they can give you work. It's not an opportunity to offer a bribe but to take responsibility and acquire the required license or certification.

You will always meet opportunities with different requirements. The requirements are there for a purpose and should encourage you to prepare your field and enlarge your vision in Christ Jesus. Let Him work on your life. Companies that meet the requirements maximize opportunities. They win tenders and contracts everywhere they bid because of their experience and qualifications. God's plan is so much bigger than our own. Once we earn a million rand we think we've made it when God has so much more in store. You might think you are too old when God is calling you to start something new.

My friend's wife was telling me about a woman who wanted to become a nurse. The odds were against her but she held on to her dream. She had no money but didn't allow that to become an excuse. She worked as a domestic worker for many years to pay her tuition. It took nine difficult years but she persevered until she made it.

Today, against all odds, she is a qualified nurse with a story to tell. My friend's wife told me that this woman is now applying for vacancies overseas. What a fruitful woman! That is what will happen with your life if you know how to prepare your field. You will change your season to a fruitful season. Make yourself available and have zeal when it comes to transforming your life. Be excited about your purpose.

Chapter Eight
Sacrifice Yourself

Since I was born I have never seen a peach tree giving birth to apples. If you see such a thing, know that the branches are not really connected to the tree. A branch bearing the wrong fruit is out of order and not in submission to the mission of the tree. The owner must cut off such a branch before it promotes the wrong kingdom by bearing the wrong fruit. The tree must produce after it's own kind and preserve it's integrity from generation to generation.

In the book of Genesis before Adam fell, the human being carried the Spirit of God in him so that he could reflect God on earth. I was not there but in my mind's eye I can see God creating Adam, smiling a little bit and saying, "That's me! That's my image." I imagine it was the same as a man who looks at his reflection in a mirror and says, "That's me!" After the fall of man God couldn't see Himself anymore in Adam because the evil one had occupied the image of God for himself. He had to ask, "Adam where are you hiding?" If I were to look at myself in the mirror and find someone else's image I would also ask as God did, "Where is my image and whose image is this now?"

The love of God doesn't give up on us. He sent Jesus to restore His image in us again. Jesus said to his disciples, "If you really love me, you will obey my commandments." He said those words to those around him at that time. He was with them in the flesh - walking and eating with them. Because he is no longer with us physically we are being instructed by the Spirit of him who died for us on the cross of Calvary - the Holy Spirit who lives in us.

So we don't do anything of our own will but in accordance with the will of Him who lives in us and causes us to bear fruit. He tells us to do this and do that and we obey Him because we are attached to Him spiritually. He gives us the power to obey. When we disobey the Holy Spirit we feel uneasy and peace leaves our hearts because we are applying for bad fruit instead of the good fruit from the true vine.

We are not here to do our own will but the will of Him who gives us our purpose for living. We are born of Him and are attached to Him spiritually. He is the vine and we are the branches. We sacrifice ourselves to please Him so that we can bear good fruit in His name. His fruits are for the good of the whole world and for us. His mission is to save the world from the hand of the enemy. If you sacrifice yourself to please Him you position yourself to be His vessel and to be used by Him. Lose yourself and be full of Him by being His hands and feet to bless the next person.

When you meet people who are troubled, sick or broken don't speak your own mind but the mind of God as a 'born again' believer. As Christians we don't do our own will but the will of our Father in Heaven. We can't do anything without being attached to Him because our life is in Him. We are in Him so that we can be the fruitful trees that He wants us to be. His will for us is to be fruitful in everything we do.

He who loves his life will lose it and he who loses his life for the Gospel will gain it. We all want to live the happy and prosperous life and God wants the same for us. He is our heart's desire. We must lose our life to please him so that our lives can be restored to us for eternity. We are branches attached to him so let us be fruitful and multiply.

We Are Not Kept By A Religious Mindset

A religious mindset is very limited and hinders God from promoting you. When God says, "Do this," you tell Him about what your grandfather said. Many born again Christians confuse religion with Christianity. They operate under the law of Moses more than by the leading of the Holy Spirit. They still believe that God hears them better when they pray on the mountains and that they will inherit the Kingdom of Heaven by their works. This is deception because our inheritance is only attained through relationship with Christ and not by our works. You might not murder, commit adultery or give false testimony but if you don't have a relationship with Christ you cannot inherit the Kingdom of Heaven. God wants the church to grow but is hindered by our contrary religious operations in His house. We must learn to build our faith on Him rather than trusting in our ability to fulfill the law.

If you consider Abraham's life you will see that he had a good and fruitful relationship with God. The practice in his times was to sacrifice animals as burnt offerings to come closer to God. When God told Abraham to ascend the mountain and sacrifice his only son Isaac this would have presented a great challenge as it was not the norm. Because Abraham had a relationship with God and was not just religious he was able to obey God and did as God said without giving religious excuses. If I was Abraham at that time my response might have been, "We don't use children for sacrifices; we use animals." Religious people will make statements like, "We don't do that in our church." They might tell you that, "We don't eat that in our clan," or, "We don't allow women to do that in our society." Even when the Lord wants to take over He is hindered by our hearts that are so full of religion that condemns us. There is no condemnation to those who trust in the Lord.

One day I was having a discussion with a sister in the Lord. She had a passion for the work of God and was telling me about her desire to play the guitar in a certain church not too far from my own. She was frustrated because she was told that women were not permitted to play instruments in that church. Culture can really limit God's work in our lives. That lady was blessed with a talent to serve the Body of Christ in that church but they missed out on the blessing because of their religious culture.

Abraham chose to walk in God's ways and not live according to the dictates of the culture he grew up in. He was faced with the same challenges that all humans are faced with but chose to prioritize his relationship with God. That is what God wants from us. He doesn't look at how many people you help, or how much you respect your mother or your father. He doesn't look at how many people you give a ride in your expensive car but He examines your relationship with Him. Do you obey Him? As a born again believer your focus should be on pleasing God and not on pleasing other people.

When you tell most people that you are a born again Christian the first thing they will do is ask you questions like, "Do you drink?" or "Do you have a girlfriend?" They expect you to be perfect in observance of the Law. They make you feel guilty even when you have done no wrong. We are saved by faith and not by works. What matters most is our relationship with God. So many people miss out on the benefits of God's grace because their mind is still trapped in religious thinking. They are governed by Law, cultural norms and the opinions of people around them. God gave the Law to the Israelites to guard them before Jesus came. We are no longer in the times of Moses times but in the times of the Holy Spirit. We must be led by the Spirit in everything we do and not by the Law.

In the book of Matthews 19:16 - 22 we read the account of the rich young ruler who asked Jesus what he had to do to inherit eternal life. Jesus replied this way, "You shall not murder, you shall not commit adultery, you shall not steal, you shall not lie, honour your mother and father and love your neighbour as you love yourself." The rich young man thought he had gotten it all right but he didn't know that Jesus had come with a new emphasis on relationship and not on the works of the Law. When Jesus told him to sell all his possessions and give the money to the poor he couldn't do it. The Bible tells us that he walked away with a sorrowful heart. Many believers are like this man - practising religion more than a relationship with Christ because religion is comfortable. The young man called Jesus "good teacher" but Jesus responded by telling him that no one is perfect except God. Religious people are always looking for mistakes everywhere and justify themselves with the Law. Jesus Christ always takes you out of your comfort zone by telling you the truth at all times. Spiritual people can be led by the Shepherd and follow by faith even into unknown territory but religious people always operate in their comfort zone. We all know that religion doesn't want new practices but instead condemns anything unfamiliar.

People still think that God is moved by works of the Law but, according to our Lord Jesus Christ, that is not the truth. He is moved by our faith and obedience in Christ.

We must have faith like Abraham and obey Him even when He says we must sacrifice our very last. That's the kind of faith He wants from us. If you obey Christ your life will never be the same. His plan makes us excel and prosper in life.

In Him we get life in abundance. In Him we live, move and conquer all. He says that the one who loses his life for Him will gain it and the one who insists on holding on to his life will lose it. If we want to gain our lives we must first lose them for Him and avail ourselves to be added to His database of labourers for the harvest is great. We must allow Him to mould us into His image.

Give Your Life For The People Around You First

Christ asked the question, "How can you love me who you can't see when you can't love people around you that you see everyday?" Those are powerful words right there. As Christians we like to say that we love Christ but we are challenged when it comes to loving the people around us. We can tithe and attend church every Sunday but, after giving our offerings, do we ever ask our neighbours who are struggling financially what they are going to eat after church or if their children have school uniforms? Do we love our spouses as we say we love Jesus? God wants us to love the people around us. That is how we are supposed to live.

The way we humble ourselves before Christ is the way we are supposed to humble ourselves before our fellow man. There was a lady named Lebu who opened a hair salon. A lady came into her salon to get her hair braided one evening when she was about to leave for a Bible study. She told the client that she couldn't assist her because she had a Bible study to go to and closed the salon. The lady tried to plead with her because it was her last chance to get her hair done before work the next morning. Lebu refused to change her position. Yes, Bible study was important but she forgot that she had a second ministry as a hair dresser. Instead of humbling herself and helping the client she proudly said, "My God comes first before you. If you can't understand that, find someone else to do your hair." Her business didn't last long because of her pride towards the people she was supposed to humbly serve. God wants us to serve our neighbours as we serve Him.

Jesus taught us that those who exalt themselves will be humbled and that those who humble themselves will be exalted. Humble yourself before your fellow men regardless of their stature and serve them beyond their expectations and the Lord will lift you up and prosper you in all your endeavours. A worshipper once said these words, "When I hold the microphone to sing a song to God I lose myself." That's the mindset that God wants from us. He wants us to lose ourselves in whatever we do to glorify Him. If you are a carpenter, do it like you are doing it for God. Lose yourself and give your best when you serve your clients. We were meant to worship God and not ourselves. We must do everything we do in accordance to His will so that His glory can be revealed in us. When we want our earthly fathers or spouses to do something for us we show appreciation. In the same way, the more we glorify God, the more He lifts us up and reveals His glory through us.

Musa Mobongwa

Chapter Nine
The Seed Of The Supernatural

We all need God's supernatural power and we can't live without it. People seem to have lost their faith in God's power but miracles still happen for those who believe and walk with Jesus Christ. He wants us to live in abundance but we must take Him at His Word and exercise our faith to see His promises manifest in our lives. When I first joined the Impact House Church family I was in pain and very vulnerable. I was on the verge of throwing in the towel. I had been hurt deeply in my former church but my new spiritual father became the miracle that I needed.

If you find a leader who preaches the pure gospel of power that makes you smile and gives you new hope and confidence, you must know that its evidence of Heaven's touch on your life. To this day I'm still born again. The supernatural power of God has transformed everything about me from the spirit realm to the physical realm. The Word of God is spirit and life. It is sharper than a double-edged sword.

We must count our blessings – no matter how small – and show gratitude for what the Lord has done. If we appreciate the small things and acknowledge that His supernatural power has done it for us, we will be able to apply our faith for the big things as well. If He healed you from a fever, you can believe for a healing from cancer. There are people who are believing for that small thing you have received. If your wife is taking your small gifts for granted how will you be inspired to buy her more gifts? It's not easy to continue giving to someone who doesn't show appreciation. If you took the healing for a headache for granted, how can you believe for a supernatural healing from cancer? If you didn't acknowledge that He promoted you to the office of supervisor by His supernatural power, how will you believe Him for a promotion to the office of CEO? We must learn to appreciate small miracles because it will grow our faith to believe for big miracles.

Appreciate Him for waking you up every morning. You could say, "Lord, if you can wake me from sleep, what can be impossible for You? Appreciate life. Appreciate your pastor, your parents, your job, your wife, your children, your husband, and your teacher. Appreciate every good thing that happens in your life. You will be provoking God's power to move on your behalf and inviting God's miracles to take place. If you are not good in mathematics, start appreciating your lecturer and the supernatural power will follow.

Be The Fruitful Tree

If you have a company, appreciate your clients. I promise you that the supernatural power will flow in your favour. If you appreciate your clients they will keep coming to buy your services. If your spiritual father appreciates you, he is provoking you to grow. The growth of the tree is in the appreciation of the roots. The tree is growing through the roots no matter how small or big, thick or thin the root is. In the same way, the root of the miracle is in the gratitude we show.

Your situation might try to blind you from seeing the goodness of God but you have to insist on being grateful. Even if you are in a broken situation spiritually or physically, I'm sure there are parts that are not broken. Write a list of the good things so that you can start to appreciate God for them. Your gratitude will help you unlock the miracle you need for the healing of the broken parts. God wants you to give Him the glory in every situation. Gratitude is the good seed that will help you to bear the fruit of supernatural miracles. God will make you fruitful in supernatural power just because you said, "Thank You." Your life will never be the same again. When you realise that all the good things you have are from the Lord your heart will overflow with gratitude. God is everywhere and all good and perfect gifts come from Him. He is faithful to believers who bear fruit in Him.

I worked in a large retail shop once where I met a woman who had been married to her husband for almost fifteen years. They loved each other but had been trying to have a child for ten years without success. I encouraged her in the Lord and I saw faith start to rise in her. As soon as I opened my mouth and said, "I see faith in you", I felt like I could help her more. I instructed her to hold her stomach and tell the Lord what she wanted. I told her that she had to first believe it in her heart then confess it with her mouth without doubting and she would fall pregnant. I was over the moon just beholding her faith and it made my faith rise too. I was so shocked when she came back to me after a few months to tell me that she was pregnant. God answered her prayer after 10 years! This experience boosted my faith in a big way and assured me that God listens and answers our prayers. He said that, "Where two or three are gathered in my name, I am there in the midst of them." He is always with us so we must just trust Him and give Him all the glory He deserves.

You don't need to add anything to help the Word work. Just speak the pure Word in the ears of one who needs a miracle. He will hear what God is saying and will get faith for his miracle. It is not hard to comfort, to motivate and to teach because you don't use your mind but just utter the words from the Bible. The Word is the seed you are supposed to deliver to the people around you so they can be supernaturally fruitful. Be the God sent angel in someone's life by giving them the Word of life. Have faith in the Word and do not doubt or entertain fear and pride. Be supernaturally motivated and walk by faith not by sight. Just say, "God said...." Have hope that things will change supernaturally if you continue focusing on what you are believing God for.

The more you focus on what you are believing for, the more the Holy Spirit will reveal mysteries to you and show you the unseen. The more you see the unseen, the more your faith grows and the more manifestation of the supernatural in your world. I believe you will start to think differently and consider the needs of the people around you more than your own. Have compassion. Hug someone. Hold someone.

Supernatural Power For Healing

Most people are looking for healing in churches and hospitals without building faith in their hearts first. You don't need to look for healing power further away than your own heart. Prepare your heart to receive the seed of God's Word for your healing. Believing starts within you - deep within your heart. Trust God to build your faith in the Word first then go to the people who can usher you to your healing. If you are sick with whatever disease or disability you still need to pursue your dreams while waiting for your healing. We are God's masterpieces whether sick or healthy. You don't need to park your dreams and wait to be healed first before you can live your life.

How can we get healed feeling sorry for ourselves? Surely healing is written in our spirit? Our names are written in the Book of Life. You cannot die before the purpose of God is fulfilled in your life. Call your healing from its hiding place. If you are a dancer, dance like you are healed. If you an author, write books and poems like you are healed. If you are an athlete, pursue your sport like you are healed. Give it your best. When I'm sick I'm healed. Take full advantage of the benefits of salvation through Christ Jesus. You will bear the fruits of healing in your life if you don't give your worries a chance. Give joy a chance instead and cease every opportunity to laugh till they name you Laughter. Take hold of the goodness of life by fire and by force.

The Fruits of Walking in Supernatural Power

When you start to walk in supernatural power, people will be in awe and wonder how you did it. Maybe you survived a fatal accident, a brutal assault, robbery, or cancer. You might have secured a million dollar business deal that no one thought you were qualified for. All of this requires supernatural power and people start to see you differently. His supernatural power kicks in where human ability and science ends. When people start to say it's over and hope is gone or the doctors start to say you are not going to make it; that is when God steps in.

The seed of supernatural power takes root in your life when you activate the Word in you. In the twenty-eighth chapter of the book of Acts we read the account of Paul on the island Malta. They were welcomed by the islanders on their arrival and shown unusual kindness. They made fire for them because it was very cold. When Paul gathered some brushwood the Bible says that a viper fastened itself to Paul's hand. When the islanders saw the snake hanging from his hand they said to each other, "This man is a murderer, for though he escaped from the sea, justice has not allowed him to live." To their surprise Paul shook the snake off into the fire and suffered no side effects from the bite. That is how people think when you are in trouble. Like the islanders, they always expect you to fall over and die. After watching Paul for a long time and seeing nothing unusual happening to him, they changed their minds and said he was a god.

Paul experienced supernatural power at work in his life. Supernatural power flows where faith is present and where there is faith you will always find the Word. I can see Paul with my mind's eye – in pain but choosing not to focus on the pain but on faith. He chose to utter the word of faith rather than uttering the complaints of pain. In whatever situation you are in, make sure you utter the word of faith so that you can experience the fruit of the supernatural taking root in you. People will start to change their minds about you. Even if the doctor's report says that tonight is your last, the Word in you is able to grace you with healing till the same doctor changes their mind.

Prayer and faith will activate supernatural power. If your business needs supernatural power, pray about it till you see something. My friend Shakes wasn't doing well in his physical science classes, but everything changed after he started to pray and ask God for wisdom and understanding. He started to see his marks getting better and better till he passed to the next grade. He did it not by his own strength but through supernatural power. He chose to pray and trust God.

If we can put our trust in God, our country would be better and we would experience transformation in everything we do. The power of the Word and prayer can transform your life. The words we speak can change atmospheres. Many can testify that since they started speaking positive words their lives have been transformed. One of my teachers told us that even if the subject is difficult we must not make that kind of confession. We should just say, "It's easy!" so that our minds can follow our words. It is the same with the Bible - you read it first then the revelation follows. There's supernatural power in the Word. One word from it can make someone's life better and open blind eyes. We must bear fruit supernaturally and allow God to use us to impact the lives of the people around us.

Conclusion

Thank God for His will and His purpose for your life because His plans are to prosper you everywhere you go and make you fruitful. Thank God that you are fruitful in Him and in His Word. The will of Him who created us is bigger than our will and our thoughts and His plans are to prosper us and not to harm us. We are the branches and He is the true vine. In Him we are fruitful spiritually, financially, physically, and even emotionally.

Since I received Jesus as my Lord and Saviour, my life has never been the same. Everywhere I go I prosper. I am surrounded by answered prayers but there are also other things that I am still waiting for. I have learnt to wait patiently in Christ Jesus as I understand that He brings all things to pass at the right time. I might feel like I need my answers immediately but His wisdom is superior and He knows better. He is like a good restaurant that offers great food. You place your order then wait patiently anticipating a delicious meal. There is no need to burn with frustration but you relax in the confidence that when the food is ready your order will be right before your eyes.

You are the fruitful tree and you inspire people around you to be fruitful as well. You are blessed and highly favoured and everything you do in obedience to His will gives birth to good fruit. You are the fruitful king and everything you ask in Jesus' name, your Father commands to reach you. He has authority over everything.

We all want success in our finances, our health, and our marriages. No one can say he doesn't want to be fulfilled or live a better life. You have come to the end of this book and it is now time to search yourself and discover who you really are. Ask yourself these questions:

- What kind of fruit are you bearing?
- What season are you in?
- Who is your leader?
- Who are your friends and are they influencing you to be fruitful?
- What are your hobbies or talent? If you don't know, examine yourself closely.

Once you have completed this exercise you will have a better idea of where you are in your life and where you need to make adjustments or do some pruning. Maybe you need to start making more fruitful friendships. You might need to change the leader you are following and find someone who will groom you in pure love. If you don't find such a leader you should consider paying for mentorship or leadership coaching. Find a church where the favour and grace of God rests.

Write your vision down and run with it. At the appointed time God will make it come to pass. I know a young man who didn't know which direction to take with his life after he matriculated. He got a scholarship to study electronics and pursued that avenue even though he didn't enjoy it. His mentor advised him to pray for the love of his new career and stop confessing how much he hated it. Instead he was advised to confess how much he loved what he did.

It is the same with marriage. The more you say you love your wife, the more your love for her will grow. Find something to do. Surround yourself with people who love what you are interested in. Such people will always speak good about it and encourage you to do it. You will see the love of it starting to develop. Be yourself. Appreciate yourself and meditate positively about your dream. Plant a seed of positivity in your heart by speaking the Word of God over your life. Speak the favour of God over your life and family even when you feel like God has forgotten you.

Be the fruitful tree.